ISBN 978-1-334-08159-0
PIBN 10689863

1 MONTH OF
FREE
READING

at
www.ForgottenBooks.com

By purchasing this book you are eligible for one month membership to ForgottenBooks.com, giving you unlimited access to our entire collection of over 700,000 titles via our web site and mobile apps.

To claim your free month visit:

www.forgottenbooks.com/free689863

English
Français
Deutsche
Italiano
Español
Português

www.forgottenbooks.com

Mythology Photography **Fiction**
Fishing Christianity **Art** Cooking
Essays Buddhism Freemasonry
Medicine **Biology** Music **Ancient
Egypt** Evolution Carpentry Physics
Dance Geology **Mathematics** Fitness
Shakespeare **Folklore** Yoga Marketing
Confidence Immortality Biographies
Poetry **Psychology** Witchcraft
Electronics Chemistry History **Law**
Accounting **Philosophy** Anthropology
Alchemy Drama Quantum Mechanics
Atheism Sexual Health **Ancient History**
Entrepreneurship Languages Sport
Paleontology Needlework Islam
Metaphysics Investment Archaeology
Parenting Statistics Criminology
Motivational

ABRAHAM LINCOLN

I was born and grew to manhood in an adjoining Coun-
.y, I attended College three years in the same county, and
vithin a very few miles of the birthplace of Abraham   Lin-
:oln, yet it never occurred to me that it would be worth the
:ime and trouble required to visit this historic place until I
1ad moved a thousand miles away.

Later, however, I had the opportunity, or rather, made
:he opportunity to visit this homestead, and as I stood   and
5azed upon the little one room log cabin in which   he   was
)oru and noted its rugged simplicity; as I viewed the   sur-
rounding country and observed that, even to   this   day,   it
loes not rank above an average in educational advantages;
as I contemplated the fact that his parents, though   good
and honest people, were wholly uneducated, and that the
father, at least was of a restless roving   disposition,   with
little ambition never accumulating any of this world's goods
aboive a very scanty subsistance; as I called to   mind   the
fact that Lincoln himself was a tall, gawky, ungainy un-
promising lad without any educational advantages; I say as
I took all these facts into consideration, I could but wonder
what characteristic or combination of   characteristics   he
possessed that would enable him, in spite of these   adverse
.conditions, to rise to the very highest office in the gift of
the American people. and to conduct the office in such manner as to cause him to become recognized by the entire civ-
ilized world as having been one of the greatest statesmun.
not only of his own age and country, but of all ages and of
all countries.

The story of the life of Lincoln would be very incomplete
without some study of the life of the sturdy pioneers   from
which he sprang.   The story of his life begins and ends   in
tragedy.   About the year 1780 his grandfather, with   his
family, consisting of a wife and five children,   three   boys
and two girls, emigratd from Virginia to Kentucky and pro-
ceeded to clear a farm in the vast wilderness, inhabited only
by the savage beasts of the forest and by the still more savage Indians that roamed at will through that part   of   the
country

Four years later while clearing land with the assistance
cf his three boys, near his little log cabin, a band of Indians
concealed in the brush nearby, shot and   killed   him.   The
eldest boy rushed to the cabin, seized the ever   ready   rifle
from its accustomed resting place above the door, and turned in time to see an Indian all decorated in war paint reach-

ıut to seize Thomas his six year old brother who
ined by the side of his dying father. Taking (
leadly aim, he fired, killed the savage ere he haı
rightened boy, who, in turn, fled to the cabin for pı

By his undaunted courage .and his superior ma
ıhip this boy—a mere lad—succeeded in holding the
ı at a safe distance until aid arrived from the nez
where Josiah, the second boy had rushed with . utr
l at the firing of the fatal shot which killed his fat.
it was that Thomas Lincoln; the father of the sub,
r discussion, was left an orphan at the tender age
ears

Not long after the occurence of this incident, there a
rated from Virginia to this part of Kentucky seve
· families, among who were Joseph and Nancy Han
brought with them young Nancy, a child of some fi
ı years

Immediately there sprang up between this little g
rhomas Lincoln an innocent, childish love which nev
red notwithstanding the fact, that Fate had so decree
they were soon to be seperated, and that they were nı
ə each other again for twelve years, at which time boı
:eached maturity.

In the meantime, Joseph Hanks sickened and die(
in the month, Nancy, the mother, overcome by grie:
passed away. Thus we see that both the father and th
er of the future President were thrown upon the meı
ıf a cold and unappreciative world at a very tender ag
the death of her parents, Nancy was taken to the hom
unıcle, and grew into womanhood in his home nea
ıethtown, Kentucky.

he was admired and courted by many of the youn
f the neighboring town, among whom were some c
ıst prominent young men of that part of the state
e had never forgotten the boy from whom she ha
əparated twelve years before.

ıe day while conversing with friends in Elizabeth
ıere appeared upon the scene the like of which ha
n seen there for years. A tall broad-shouldere
man with deerskin breeches tucked in the top of hi
ıe boots, an old fashioned rifle in one hand and a ki
ınter tools in the other, on his head a coon skin ca·
ə rear of which still protruded the tail of the anima
ıich the cap was made. Truly not an imposing figʋr
cy Hanks immediately rushed from the crowd o
ıen, dressed in broadcloth though they were, to th
ıe newcomer, for it was none other than Thoma
the lover of her childhood days.

of these admirers, a man of wealth and position
upon her to forsake her lover and marry him, bu
il. According to the records of the County Clerk'

office of Washington County, Kentucky, a certified copy of which I have in my possession. these two, the parents of Abraham Lincoln, were united in matrimony, on June 12, 1806. Here, out of respect of the memory of Nancy Hanks as well as that of her illustrious son, I feel that duty compels me to mention one thing that I would prefer to leave buried with the dead, and I offer as my only excuse for allowing it to enter this discussion, is the fact that almost every one with whom I have talked upon the subject have heard the damaging charges.

Some have never heard the charge disputed, and therefore believe it to be true. Others will say they have heard it disputed but frankly say they do not know whether it is true or not. During one of Lincoln's heated political campaigns, some person for whom I do not find suitable words in the English language to express my contempt, made the charge that Lincoln's birth was not an honorable one Immediately the false accusation was spread throughout the land. His friends, among whom was the Hon. Henry Watterson, though a political enemy, took upon themselves the task of making a personal investigation, and proved beyond a shadow of doubt that the charge was as false as the heart of the infamous individual who made it. More than three quarters of a century have been recorded on the scroll of time since this damnable lie was started; more than a hundred years have passed since the death of this sainted mother to whom Lincoln said he owed all that he was or ever hoped to be. and though it has been proven to be absolutely false. yet after all this lapse of time there are many who still believe it to be true.

Oh how easy it is, by some trifling remark, some exaggerated insinuation of some direct charge, to injure or disrupt the reputation of the best of men or the purest of women, but oh how difficult it is to rebuild that reputation when once destroyed.

Lincoln on an occasion said, "Die when I may, I want it said of me by those who knew me best that I always plucked a thistle and planted a flower wherever I thought a flower would grow."

If all men and all women would act in accordance with the thought expressed in this sentence, many a tear would remain unshed, many a good and noble heart would remain unbroken. The first year of the married life of the Lincoln's was spent in Elizabethtown where Sarah the oldest child was born. Shortly after the birth no doubt, on account of poverty and partly on account of the animosity he had aroused by his persistent antagonism to slavery, he removed to a little farm thirteen miles away near the town of Hodgensville. It was here in the little log cabin which still stands, that Abraham was born Feb. 12, 1809.

The boyhood days of Lincoln were spent very much as

were the days of other boys of the time with this notable exception. At this early date, game of all kinds was **plen**tiful and it was the special delight of most boys to spend their leisure moments in hunting. Not so with Lincoln. He was adverse to taking life in any manner, therefore hunting had no attraction for him, and so we find him at a very early age, devoting his leisure moments to study.

There were no educational advantages in those days. According to his own testimony all the schooling he received in the school room did not exceed ten or twelve months and, under teachers who made no pretensions toward teaching anything beyond the three "R's". Not on account of these early disadvantages but in spite of them by his **un**tiring and persistent application to study, he succeeded in acquiring a fairly good education.

As we have said before the father was of a restless, roving disposition so we find him becoming dissatisfied with his little home in Kentucky. In the fall of 1816, he moved to Spencer County Indiana where he again experienced the hardships of frontier life. Here it was that Nancy Hanks Lincoln sickened and died.

It became the painful duty of the husband to go into the forest, cut down one of the gigantic trees which grew in abundance, saw it into lumber with the old fashioned whipsaw, and manufacture the coffin in which she was laid to rest.

In due time, realizing that his children needed the guiding hand of a mother, he returned to Kentucky and married a Mrs. Johnson a lady with whom he was acquainted before either was married. A warm friendship grew up between her and young Abraham, and she being an educated and cultured lady for that day and time, there is little doubt that she exerted over him an influence which had much to do in preparing him for the high position in life to which he was to be called.

About the time of Lincoln's 21st birthday, the father was again seized with the wander-lust, this time wending his way northward traveling by ox-team and wagon, one of them being driven by Abraham himself. They settled near New Salem, some 15 miles from Springfield, Ill., where the father and son built a log cabin, made rails and fenced ten acres of land, and placed it under cultivation the first year.

A trader of the community seeing Lincoln's robust build and almost giant strength, and having implicit confidence in his honesty, employed him for the paltry sum of

$8.00 per month to build a boat, and loading it with such goods and povisions as would find ready sale at the various plantations, sent him and another youth down the Illinois river to the Mississippi and down this river to New Orleans.

I will burden you with but one incident of that or rather a preceeding voyage. One night while anchored at the water's edge, being wrapped in peaceful slumber they were attacked by seven stalwart negroes whose object was to murder them and take possession of their goods. By their superior strength and skill however they succeeded in vanquishing their assailants with only slight injury to themselves and cutting anchor drited on down the river in safety. Thirty years later these same negroes, if alive, together with four million of their race, received their freedom at the hands of him whom they sought to murder.

The rest of the trip was made in safety and after having disposed of all their stores they returned part of the way by steamboat and part of the way on foot. Upon his arrival home he accounted for every penny of the money taken in, and thus built a reputation for honesty which, no doubt, had much to do with his future success.

After working in the store of the man for whom he had made his voyage down the river, he and a man by the name of Berry bought a store from the Herndon Brothers, giving their promissory note in payment for same. Tho unknown to them at the time they made the purchase, the store was on the verge of bankruptcy. The business failed, and Berry fled leaving the whole responsibility on Lincoln who though not able to pay at the time, assumed not only his debt but also that of his worthless partner, a debt which took him seventeen years to liquidate. This debt could not have been collected by law, yet this man whose honesty I have never heard questioned, paid it to a farthing with interest, thus again demonstrating that he was a man in whom the most implicit confidence could be placed. On May 7, 1833 he was appointed post-master of New Salem, a position which he held until 1836 when New Salem seems to have disappeared and the post office was moved to a neighboring town. Again thrown out of employment he faced the most critical period of his history, for he realized as all men who ever reach any marked degree of success must sooner or later realize, that in order to accomplish anything worth while he must specialize in one particular line of industry.

His natural inclination was toward the study of law, but on account of his lack of education he hesitated, fearing that he could not compete with the more highly educated lawyers of his time. As we look back over the brilliant accomplishments of his future life, it is amusing, indeed, to think that he hesitated for two years in a choice between the profession of law and the trade of a blacksmith. Had

a oss to himself and to his country. I someti
think that other men, if not all men, are created for so
specific line of work and that if they use their time in pr
aration, and hold themselves in readiness to do that wo
the Divine Creator in His own time and in his own w
will point the proper proceedure for the accomplishment
this work. I believe this was true in the case of Abraha
Lincoln. Prior to his appointment as Postmaster at Ne
Salem, to be more exact in the year 1832 at the age of
he entered the race for the legislature, and tho he was litt
known outside of his immediate community, and tho he ha
only ten days in which to make a canvass of the distric
and notwithstanding, the fact that he was defeated, he mad
a showing for which he had no reason to be ashamed.
might add that this was the only time in his history that h
met defeat at the hands of the people.

Two years later,, encouraged by the vote, he had re
ceived at the previous election, he again entered the
race and was elected. Being brought into contact with
men more highly educated than any with whom he had ever
before associated and having plenty of spare time for study,
and receiving encouragement from his associates, he decided
to begin the study of law.

He was re-elected in the elections of 36-38 and 40 at
the end of which he voluntarily retired It cannot be said
that he made a specially brilliant record during his career
as a legislator; yet he must have stood well with his col-
leagues for at the last two terms of which he was a member
he was the choice of his party for speaker, but being in the
minority, he of course was defeated.

Upon his retirement from the legislature he devoted his
entire time to the study and practice of law; though it is
true that in conventions which nominated candidates for
Congress in the year 1842 and also in 1844 he was an aspir-
ant for that office.

Two years later his political aspirations were gratified
as he was elected and took his seat as a member of the thir-
tieth congress. Here as in the Legislature he did not dis-
play any unusual ability but was a hard worker and stood
firm for his convictions.

I shall not deal extensively with his congressional record
but there is one thing I cannot refrain from mentioning because it shows the trend of his mind at that early date and
because it leads up to some of his great deeds in after life.
The slavery question was becoming one of national promi-

nence. It was agitated in the minds of the leaders of both north and south. The issues between them were so clearly drawn that any one could understand. The North demanded that slavery be confined to the States in which it already existed, the South claimed that it could be lawfully extended to any part of the country. In all the history of Lincoln which I have read I do not find a single instance in which he claimed that Congress had any constitutional right to prohibit slavery in the states where it already existed. Maryland and Virginia were both slave states. They had ceded to the federal government a strip of land on either side of the Potomac as a location of the National Capital, and in doing so gave up all rights they had as states, and it naturally fell under the jurisdiction of the National Congress.

According to Lincoln's own statement there had been maintained for fifty years within sight of the windows of the Capital, a sort of negro livery stable, where droves of negroes were collected, temporarily kept, and finally taken to southern markets, precisely like droves of horses. His very nature revolted at this traffic in human lives.

He already entertained the idea which he later, during his term as president, urged upon both houses of Congress, that the only just mode of getting rid of the institution of slavery was by a system of compensated emancipation, giving freedom to the slave and a money indemnity to the owner. Believing this to be the only just and consistent way of settling the controversy he introduced in congress a carefully prepared bill providing for the abolishment of slavery in the District of Columbia upon the following terms:-

First: That the laws should be adopted by a popular vote in the district.

Second: A temporary system of apprenticeship and gradual emancipation for children born of slave mothers after January 1, 1850.

Third: The government to pay cash value for slaves voluntarily manumitted by their owners.

Fourth: Prohibiting bringing slaves into the District or selling them out of it.

Fifth: Providing that government officers, citizens of slave states might bring with them and take away again their slave house-servants.

Sixth: Leaving the existing fugitive-slave law in force.

In spite of the justice and simplicity of this bill, in spite of the fact that a majority of the citizens of the District were anxious for its passage, the bill was never allowed to come to a vote.

Mr. Lincoln retired at the close of the term, and resumed the practice of law. For a time he seems to have lost all interest in politics, and no doubt would have spent the remainder of his life in the practice of law, had not congress at this time repealed the famous Missouri Compromise Bill which again threw both North and South into a feverish heat of excitement and which according to Lincoln's own words, aroused him as he had never been aroused before.

The repeal of the Missouri Compromise was not effected until May 1850 and from that time till the elections th following fall, intense excitement prevailed throughout the country. Upon two previous occasions that great peace-loving statesman, Henry Clay, by his supreme eloquence had succeeded in having a bill passed which for a time lulled to rest the passions of his countrymen, thus postponing for a time the war that inevitably must come. The time had almost if not quite arrived when the issue would down at no man's bidding. Lincoln seems to have taken no part in the public discussions until September following the repeal of the Missouri Compromise in May, though it may be assumed that he used the intervening time in study and preparation for the Herculean task which he later voluntarily took upon himself. Excitement ran high everywhere: men who had been lifelong friends were at dagger's point. In some cases members of the same family were at each other's throat. The time had passed when it was within the power of any man to allay the passions of the different factions. With this state of affairs existing and with the regular elections coming on we find the most prominent leaders of all factions assembling at the fair grounds at Springfield, Illinois. Judge Steven A. Douglas, the leading factor in the repeal of the Missouri Compromise, had an appointment to speak on that occasion and in their search for some one to oppose him the opposition unanimously selected Abraham Lincoln. Truly two great intellects had clashed.

Douglass was known throughout the Country as an able and forceful speaker. Lincoln at that time was scarcely known outside the borders of his own state. As to who got the better of this debate and the others which followed will be determined by each individual according to whether he is in sympathy with the one or the other. At any rate so convincing were his arguments so forcible his language that Lincoln, quite unexpected to himself, immediately found himself thrust forward as a power in national politics. Some of the ideas expressed in those debates will live as long as the world stands.

In his Peoria speech in speaking of the slavery question he used the following language:

I hate Slavery because of the monstrous injustice of

slavery itself. I hate slavery because it deprives our republican example of its just influence in the world; enables the enemies of free institutions, with plausibility, to taunt us as hypocrites; causes the real friends of freedom to doubt our sincerity, and especially because it forces so many good men among ourselves into an open war with the very fundamntal principals of civil liberty, criticizing the Declaration of Independence, and insisting that there is no right principal or action but self-interest.....Slavery is founded in the selfishness of man's nature, opposition to it in his love of justice

These principles are an eternal antagonism and when brought into collision so fiercely as slavery extension brings them, shakes and throes and convulsions must ceaselessly follow. Repeal the Missouri Compromise, repeal all compromises, repeal the Declaration of Independence, repeal all past history, you still cannot repeal human nature. It still will be the abundance of man's heart that slavery extension is wrong, and out of the abundance of his heart his mouth will continue to speak.

Again he said:

"The doctrine of self-government is right—absolutely and etrnally right but it has no just application as here attempted. Or perhaps I shoud rather say, that whether it has such application depends upon whether a negro is not or is a man. If he is not a man, in that case, he who is a man may as a matter of self-government do just what he pleases with him, but if the negro is a man, is it not to that extent a total destruction of self government to say that he too shall not govern himself? When the white man governs himself and also governs another man, that is more than self-government—that is despotism."

I particularly object to the new position which the avowed principal of this Nebraska law gives to slavery in the body politic. I object to it because it assumes that there can be moral right in the enslaving of one man by another. I object to it as a dangerous alliance for a free people, a sad evidence that, feeling prosperity, we forget right; that liberty as a principal we have ceased to revere. Little by little but steadily as man's march to the grave, we have been giving up the old for the new faith. Near eighty years ago we began by declaring that all men are created equal; but now from that beginning we have run down to the other declaration that for some men to enslave others, is a "sacred right of self-government." These principals cannot stand together. They are as opposite as God and Mammon."

Again on another occasion he used the following forcible language:

"A house divided against itself cannot stand." I believe this government cannot endure permanently, half slave and half free. I do not expect the Union to be dissolved—

I do not expect the house to fall but I do expec
to be divided.   It will become all one thing (r
Either the opponents of slavery   will   arrest
spread of it, and place it where the public min(
in the belief that it is in course of ultin.ate e
its advocates will push forward till it shall b
in all the States, old as well as   new, .North
South.   '

Little did he dream at this time that in his
be placed the power, and upon his shoulders tl
bility of determining whether or not slavery sh(
exist.   We will pass rapidly over the succeedi1
the next Presidential election.

Though he was almost the last man to reali:
become by his able discussion of the slavery que
ure of national prominence. Almost a year befo1
ing of the National convention an enthusiastic fr
itor of one of the leading papers of Illinois, had
permission to announce him a candidate for the
but Lincoln discouraged such action by answeri1
tainly am flattered and gratified that some par
think of me in that connection; but I really thin
for our cause that no concerted effort such as yo
should be made."

As the time of the meeting of the convention
a body of influential friends waited upon him a
that he allow them to enter his name in the con
he finally agreed to do, not with any hope of sec
coveted prize, but believing that if he could mak
erable showing of strength in the convention, it
able him to secure a senatorship of his state.   Li1
high with the citizenship of his own state so the 1
at Springfield as delegates to the national convent
cago, were his friends and were men of ability t
able to exert a great influnee in his behalf amon
gates at the National Convention.   Lincoln did
the Chicago convention humorously saying that h
much of a candidate to attend and not enough o
late to stay away.

The delegates assembled in the Wigwam, a la
ary building erected especially for the purpose.
lttle doubt that William H. Seward was th
hoice of a majority of the members of the conv
n account of his strong anti-slavery views he h;
bnoxious to a few of the pivotal states; thus mal

feat c.. .ain in case of .iis nomination. Lincoln was anti-slavery but not an abolitionist. Each had a strong following. The balloting began on the third day. The first ballot gave Seward 173½ votes, Lincoln 102, the remainder going to favorite sons of different states. Evidently the battle was between these two. On second the delegation of various states after having cast a complimentary vote for their favorite, began to drift to the one or the other of the leading candidates.

The close of the second ballot disclosed the fact that Seward had received 184 votes and Lincoln 181, and a burst of applause which was checked with difficulty by the chairman, shook the building to its very foundation. Quiet being restored, and after a hasty and excited consultation of various vote delegations, the third ballot began, and after counting up the votes it was found that Lincoln had 321½, Seward 180. Two hundred and thirty three votes being necessary to a choice, it was observed that Lincoln was with-in 11½ votes of the nomination. A death-like quiet prevailed in the room, each wondering what the next move would be. They had not long to wait, for David K. Carter sprang from his seat and reported the change of 4 Ohio votes from Chase to Lincoln.

Pandimonium broke loose, meen cheered, cannons roared and telegraph wires spread the news through the country that Lincoln the rail splitter was the nominee for president of the United States. In the meantime the Democratic party assembled in convention and found themselves hopelessly divided on the slavery question. One faction nominated Judge Douglas who regarded slavery as being purely a state question, and that each state had right to accept or reject it as they saw fit. Another faction, the Buchanan, declared slavery to be right and beneficial, and pledging its extension, nominated John C. Breckenridge of Kentucky. Still another faction ignoring the question entirely nomiated John Bell of Tennessee. These four entered the battle for the Presidency which resulted in the election of Abraham Lincoln.

Even before his inauguraton war clouds hung ominously on the horizon. This being intended as a discourse on the life of Lincoln and not a discussion of the civil war; and having neither time nor the inclination to bring before you the many unpleasant happenings of that terrific struggle, I shall content myself with mentioning only those things which have a tendency to portray the beauties and nobleness of character in the life of him whom I am so feebly trying to eulogize. Much as I admire, love and honor the memory of Lincoln, I say to you frankly that I would rather

rom my body, rather than knowingly,
him, utter one word that would cast a
honesty, integrity or courage of the
ith who opposed him.

he North and those of the South had
irely different environments. Those
wn up surrounded by slavery which was
tioned by the national Government, un-
very as an inalienable right with which
ien, had a right to interfere.

ind, those of the North not coming in
slavery, and no doubt hearing many ex-
f cruelties prepetrated on the slaves of
and believing that slavery had no place
ose very foundation rock was built upon
ill men are created free and equal,"
least to prevent its spreading to states
st.

ditions existing, and with the two fac-
war Abraham Lincoln was inaugurated
ted States at the most critical period of

sire was to avoid war. In substantia-
ote from his inaugural address, in which
nest plea against the folly of disunion
itaining peace and fraternal good will,
g language:
: our country believes slavery is right
ended, while the other believes it is
t be extended; that is the only substan-
ially speaking, we cannot separate. We
espective sections from each other, and
ve wall between them. A husband and
l and go out of the presence and beyond
ier; but the differnt parts of our coun-
They cannot but remain face to face,
er amicable or hostile must continue
possible, then, to make that intercourse
ir more satisfactory after separation
iens make treaties easier than friends
n treaties be more faithfully enforced
laws can among friends? Suppose you
it fight always; and when, after much
d no gain on either you cease fighting,
stions as to terms of intercourse are
Your hands, my dissatisfied fellow-
in mine, is the momentous issue of
rnment will not assail you. You can
iout being yourselves the aggressors. I
are not enemies, but friends. We must
iugh passion may have strained, it
onds of affection."

But war was on and it was beyond the power of any man to stop it. I question if there was a man in Lincoln's cabinet who in the start, did not believe himself to be superior to his chief, and better able to grapple with the mighty questions that constantly come up for adjustment, but there never was a time, from the day he took his seat until the day he died at the hand of a cowardly assassin that he did not have complete control of the situation.

He was born a leader, and though ever ready to advise with the members of his cabinet, he reserved unto himself the final decision of all important questions. The first to have this fact forcibly thrust upon him was Mr. Seward, Secretary of State. Barely a month had elapsed after the inauguration of Mr. Lincoln, when Mr. Seward handed him a document entitled, "Some thoughts for the president's consideration." Never in all history before or since has such instrument of writing passed between a cabinet officer and his chief. We have not space to give the note in full but it said in substance, Mr. President you have reached the end of the first month of your administration, and are yet without a policy, either domestic or foreign. The administration should cease talking about slavery and emphasize the question of union or disunion. You should demand an explanation of France and Spain, and if they do not give satisfactory replies you should convene congress and declare war on them at once. But whatever policy we adopt, there must be an energetic prosecution in it. For this purpose it must be somebody's business to pursue and direct it incessantly. Either the President must do it himelf, and be all the while active in it. or devolve it on some member of his cabinet. Once adopted, debate on it must end, and all agree and abide. It is not in my especial province. But, neither seek to evade nor assume responsibility.

Could you for a moment imagine a more egotistic or insulting letter. Most men under similar circumstances would have become enraged, and answered with the most abusive language at his command. Not so with Lincoln.

In spite of the glowing insult this diamond in the rough this uneducated scholar, this even tempered statesman, with out the least show of resentment, and with cool head and a calm heart, answered that letter that very night, as only a statesman of the highest and noblest character could have answered.

Not a word needed to be added, and not a word could have been left unsaid without lessening its effect as a whole. It is worth repeating if for no other reason than to show how a great man conducts himself under trying circumstances. I read his answer:

EXECUTIVE MANSION; April 1, 1861.—Hon. W. H.

Seward—My Dear Sir: Since parting with you I have been considering your paper dated this day and entitled "some thoughts for the President's consideration." The first proposition in it is, "we are at the end of a month's administration and yet are without a policy, either domestic, or foreign."

At the beginning of that month in the inaugural I said "The power confided to me will be used to hold, occupy and possess the property and places belonging to the Government, and to collect the duties and imports'. This had your approval at the time; and taken in connection with the order I immediately gave General Scott, directing him to employ every means in his power to strengthen and hold the forts, comprises the exact domestic policy you urge, with the single exception that it does not propose to abandon Fort Sumter.

The news received yesterday in regard to Santo Domingo certainly brings a new item within the range of our foreign policy, but up to that time we have been preparing circulars and instructions to ministers and the like all in perfect harmony without even a suggestion that we had no foreign policy.

Upon your closing proposition That "Whatever policy we adopt there must be an energetic prosecution of it.

"For this purpose it must be somebody's business to pursue and direct it incessantly.

Either the President must do it himself, and be all the while acitve in it, or devolve it upon some member of his cabinet.

"Once adopted, debates must end, and all agree and abide." I remark that if this be done, I must do it. When a general line of policy is adopted,I apprehend there is no danger of its being changed without good reason, or continuing to be a subject of unnecessary debate. Still upon points arising in its progress, I wish, and suppose I am entitled to have the advice of all the Cabinet.

Your obedient servant,
A Lincoln.

So kind, yet so consclusive was the argument that Mr. Seward stepped back into his place, no doubt realizing that Λr. Lincoln was fully capable of conducting his own affairs and so far as is known neither ever referred to the correspondence again.

As further evidence of the fact that Seward realized that he had come in contact with a real leader of men, . In speaking of a Cabinet meeting a short time after, he said there was but one vote cast and that was by Lincoln. It is true that he took upon himself the responsibility of deciding all important questions during the entire war, not shifting it upon any other man's shoulders, never wavering from what he believed to be right.

Another matter of continuous annoyance between him and members of his Cabinet, as well as some of the leading generals of the army was what they pleased to term his abuse of the pardoning power. With all his strength and power, his heart was as tender as that of a woman, so much so that he granted many pardons almost if not entirely, without apparent reason. This proceedure was strongly opposed by those in command of the army who claimed it to be impossible to maintain obedience to the rules and regulatns of the army, so long as such leniency was extended to the transgressors of those rules and regulations.

It is said that on one occasion a commander actually cut the wire leading from the Executive Mansion to his office in order to prevent executive clemency being extended some prisoners who had been condemned to death. This lovely trait of his character is beautifully portrayed in the story told by Mr. John B. Ally of Boston who having occasion to visit the White House on three consecutive days noticed, on each occasion an old white haired man waiting in an outer hall silently weeping. The third day, touched by the sad spectacle, he accosted the man, and ascertained that he had a son sentenced to death, and was trying to reach the President. "Come along," said Ally "and I will take you to the President." Mr. Lincoln listened patiently to the old man's story, and with tears in his own eyes, replied, that he had just received a telegram from the commanding General imploring him not to interfere. The broken hearted old man, believing all was lost, cast a last despairing look at the President and started toward the door. Ere he had eached it however, the President called him back, and said, "The General may telegraph and telegraph, but I am going to pardon that young man". He immediately sent a dispatch directing that sentence be suspended until such a time as he himself should order execution. Upon hearing this, the old man again burst into tears, exclaiming between sobs, "Mr. President, that is not a pardon, you merely hold up the sentence of my boy until you can order him to be shot." Lincoln turned quickly and in a tender voice calculated to allay his gravest fears said: "Go along, old man, go in peace. If your son lives till I order him shot he will live to be as old as Methuselah."

Time will not permit me to enumerate the many similar incidents in his life, for they were of almost daily occurrence. Always showing strength and power, yet ever tempering justice with sympathy and tolerance.

A beautiful trait of his character is very forcibly brought out in his letter to his step brother, who it seems, was continually calling upon him for pecuniary aid. I am going to read this letter not because it contains any special value from a literary standpoint, but because of the vital truths expressed therein, truths just as applicable to life today as in the days of Lincoln and will be just as applicable to life fifty or a hunred years hence, as it is today. Here is the letter:

Springfield, Jan. 2, 1851—Dear Brother: Your request for eighty dollars I do not think it best to comply with. At the various times I have helped you a little you have said: "We can get along very well now.', but in a short time I find you in the same difficulty again. Now this can only happen through some defect in you. What that defect is I think I know. You are not lazy, and still you are an idler. I doubt whether since I saw you, you have done a good, whole day's work, in any one day. You do not very much dislike to work, and still you do not work much, merely because it does not seem to you you get enough for it. This habit of uselessly wasting time is the whole difficulty. It is vastly important to you, and still more to your children that you break the habit.

You are now in need of some money, and what I propose is that you go to work "tooth and nail", for somebody who will give you money for it. Let father and your boys take charge of your things at home, prepare for a crop and make the crop, and you go work for the best money wages you can get, or in discharge of any debt you owe, and to secure you a fair reward for your labor, I promise you that for every dollar you will get for your labor between this and the 1st of May, either in money or on your indebtedness I will then give you one other dollar. By this if you hire yourself for ten dollars a month, from me you will get ten dollars more, making twenty dollars.

In this I do not mean that you shall go off to St. Louis or the lead mines in Missouri, or the gold mines in California, but I mean for you to go at it for the best wages you can get close to home in Coles County. If you will do this you will soon be out of debt, and, what is better, you will have acquired a habit which will keep you from getting in debt again. But if I should now clear you out of debt, next year you would be just as deep in debt as ever.

You say you would almost give your place in Heaven for seventy or eighty dollars? Then you value your place in Heaven very cheap, for I am sure you can, with the offer I make, get the seventy or eighty dollars for four or five months work.

You said if I will lend you the money, you will deed me the land and if you don't pay the money back, you will deliver possession. Nonsense; if you cannot now live with the land, how will you then live without it?

You have always been kind to me, and I do not mean to be unkind to you. On the contrary, if you will but follow my advice, it will be worth eighty times eighty dollars to you.

Affectionately your brother,

A. Lincoln

Any young man of ordinary intelligence who will closely study the contents of this letter and put the thoughts therein expressed into practice will scarcely fail to succeed.

Mr. Lincoln, so far as I have been able to read never at any time, claimed any constitutional right, or expressed a desire to free the slaves in states where it lawfully existed, except by the consent of the owners, or without what he believed to be a just remuneration.

He had, however, naturally considered, and in his own mind adopted a plan of dealing with the question, the same plan he had introduced in congress for dealing with slavery in the District of Columbia. The plan of compensated abolishment. The little state of Delaware contained within its boundary only 1798 slaves. The President proposed through the representative of that State a scheme for the gradual emancipation of the 1798 slaves, on the payment of the United States government, at the rate of $400.00 for each slave in annual installments extending over a period of thirty one years. He believed that if he could induce one state to adopt the plan, its feasibility would be proven, and that other states would likewise adopt it. The law makers of the State of Delaware saw fit to reject the proposition.

Not discouraged by defeat, the President, a short time later sent a special message to congress in which he recommended the adoption of the following resolution:

"RESOLVED, That the United States ought to cooperate with any state which may adopt gradual abolishment of slavery, giving to such State pecuniary aid, to be used by such state, in its discretion, to compensate for the inconveniences public and private, produced by such change of system."

Though the resolution was adopted by both Houses of Congress its terms were never accepted by any slave state. In answer to objections made by opponents of the resolutions, who believed in the plan to be too expensive, Lincoln used the following forcible language. "Less than one half day's cost of this war would pay for all the slaves in Delaware at four hundred dollars per head. Less than eighty seven days cost of this war would at the same price pay for all in Delaware, Maryland, District of Columbia, Kentucky and Missouri." I might add that one does not have to be an expert historian to know that by adding the indirect cost of the war such as pensions etc., to the original cost, enough

money has been paid out to have bought ever⌃ slave i
union and still have a large surplus left.

From the time war was declared until the day o
death the slavery question was of secondary conside.
to Lincoln, his main object, in fact his only object, be
save the union which he had sworn to preserve and d
If you doubt this statement I have but to refer you t
remark to Alexander H. Stephens, vice president o:
Southern Confederacy, who was one of the delegate⌃
pointed to confer with the national authorities to ѕ
some means could not be devised to restore peace. I
the conference which came to naught, Lincoln hande
...⌃ a blank sheet of paper and said, "Stephens i⌃
will let me write "union" at the top of that page, yo⌃
write below it whatever you please."

Again if you still have a doubt that his motive ⌃
save the Union and not destroy slavery read his lett
Horace Greeley under date of Aug. 22, 1862.

"As to the policy I seem to be pursuing, as you
have not meant to leave any one in doubt.

I would save the Union. I would save it the s⌃
way under the Constitution. The sooner the national
ority can be restored, the nearest the Union will be
Union as it was. If there be those who would not ѕa
Union unless they could at the same time save slaver⌃
not agree with them. If there be those who would nc
the Union unless they could, at the same time, destrc
very, I do not agree with them. My paramount obj
this struggle is to save the Union, and is not either t
or destroy slavery. If I could save the Union withou⌃
ing any slaves, I would do it, if I could save it by free⌃
the slaves, I would do it; and if I could save it by f
some and leaving others alone I would also do that.
I do about slavery and the colored race, I do because
lieve it helps to save the Union, and what I forbear, ⌃
bear because I do not believe it will save the Uni
shall do less whenever I shall believe what I am
hurts the cause, and I shall do more whenever I sha⌃
lieve doing more will help the cause. I shall try to ⌃
errors when shown to be errors, and I shall ado⌃
views so fast as they shall appear to be true views.

I have here stated my purpose according to my v
official duty; and I intend no modification of my ⌃
pressed wish that all men everywhere could be free.

Yours,

A Lincoln

On September 22, 1862, after long and careful t⌃
believing the time had come when the freedom ⌃

slave would add to chance for success of the Northern Army he exercised his right as a war measure, issuing a proclamation that in all states wherein rebellion still existed on Jan 1, 1863, all slaves should then and forever be free. So on this memorable Jan. 1, the states still being in a state of war, he issued his final emancipation proclamation freeing the slaves of the entire country.

Do you doubt for a moment that it was his intention to pay for those slaves; if so then listen, on Feb. 5, 1865, just 69 days prior to the day of his death when the final result of the war must have been apparent to all, he called his Cabinet together, and read them a draft of resolution and proclamation embodying his idea, offering the Southern states four hundred million dollars, a sum equal to the cost of the war for two hundred days, on condition that hostilities cease by the first day of April. The Cabinet unanimously disagreed with him, however, and he very reluctantly laid the matter aside.

I want to say to you here the greatest blow that ever befell the South was when Abraham Liscoln fell, at the hands of a cowardly assasin, for had he lived, during the reconstruction days, the South would have received many advantages, which they did not receive under changed administration, one of which would have been payment for every slave set free. Not wishing to burden you with a further discussion of the subject, I now invite you to accompany me to the City of Washington, and witness the last tragedy in the life of this illustrious statesman. The war is practically over. Lee has surrendered, and all Washington, if not the whole country, is rejoicing in the hope of an early peace.

It is April 14th, that season of the year when all nature has taken on new life. At noon of this memorable day it becomes known throughout the City, that the President would visit Ford's Theatre in the evening. General Grant and wife are in the City, and are invited by Mrs. Lincoln to accompany the Presidential party as guests of honor. They accept. but at the last moment are called out of the City, and Mrs. Li coln then invited Major Rathborne and fiancee Miss Harris, instead. Being detained by visitors, the play had made some progress when the party appeared. The band strikes up, "Hail to the Chief", the actors cease for a moment, the audience rises, and cheers tumultuusly the President bowing in acknowledgment takes his seat in his box with the rest of the party and the play goes merrily on. I leave you here, oh noble soul that you are, to enjoy as best you can the few remaining moments of a well spent life, for as I shift the scenery to another part of the City I see forming against you a conspiracy the awfulness of which makes my very blood turn cold. In the house of

...he weeks previous, for the purpose of assassi---

y the president, but several members of his

. Let us say here that the South had noth-

this conspiracy. At the very moment Lin-

g such a heart felt ovation at the theatre, we

s Booth, the leader of the conspiracy a young

sessing appearance, enter a livery stable and

t fleet-footed animal to be had. He rides up

the theatre every part of which is familiar

ng an actor, and leaving his horse in charge

enters a nearby saloon and takes a drink of

ess to strengthen his nerves for the dastardly

but to commit. I see him enter the theatre,

tendants and actors, causing no suspicion,

miliar figure around there. All are intensely

e play consequntly no one observes him as he

toward the President's Box.

a card to the attendant and is allowed to

me to digress long enough to remark that

re congregated, the life of each proved to be

in itself, for be it known that one was to die

n of another day, one was to be hunted from

and finally shot while a barn was burning

while another was to pass her remaining days

and sadness over the tragic death of her hus-

two lovers one was to slay the other and later

ving maniac. But again to the picture. As

coward enters the box, I see him draw from

evolver, from the other a long dangerous

ody being intensely interested in the play on

ne notices the horrible scene being enacted in

Placing the revolver close to the back of the

d he fires. Quickly Major Rathborne springs

e him, and receives a severe knife wound in

eized the audience, everybody realizing that

astrophe has happened, yet, at the time not

it is. Amid this confusion the chief actor in

shes to the rear and with a single bound

ge. As I gaze upon the picture it seems that

sion, he will make his escape without hinder-

Supreme power intervenes, for as he rushes

can Flag, with which the stage is decorated,

and he is thrown violently to the floor,

b in the fall. In spite of this accident how-

s the rear of the building, and ·mounting ·

his steed rides rapidly away into the night.

We have not the time to follow as he is pursued from place to place, until he is finally surrounded and shot in a burning barn. The President lingered, unconsciously until dawn of the following day when he quietly passes into eternity loved, honored and respected by all.

Let me say in conclusion especially to the youth of the country, you cannot all be called to fill high positions in life such as Lincoln was called, but you can fill your position in life whatever it may be with honesty and efficiency You can pluck a thistle and plant a flower wherever you think a flower will grow. You can be true to yoursef, to your country and to your God, in doing these things you will be an asset to whatever community you choose to cast your lot.

Last but not least, when you have righteously fulfilled your mission in this life and find yourself confronted by that grim monster, death, there will be an outstretcted hand ready to guide you across to the other shore where all your trials and troubles will come to an end. and where all will be peace and happiness forever and forever.

CPSIA information can be obtained
at www.ICGtesting.com
Printed in the USA
BVHW060916140119
537775BV00010B/2260/P